Shift Work

SOUTHERN MESSENGER POETS

Dave Smith, *Series Editor*

Shift Work

POEMS

Bobby C. Rogers

Louisiana State University Press

BATON ROUGE

Published by Louisiana State University Press
lsupress.org

LSU Press Paperback Original

DESIGNER: *Mandy McDonald Scallan*
TYPEFACE: *Minion*

Street Arrows, 1973, by Walker Evans. Copyright © Walker Evans Archive, The Metropolitan Museum of Art. Purchase, Samuel J. Wagstaff Jr. Bequest and Lila Acheson Wallace Gift, 1994.

Library of Congress Cataloging-in-Publication Data
Names: Rogers, Bobby C. (Bobby Caudle), author.
Title: Shift work : poems / Bobby C. Rogers.
Description: Baton Rouge : Louisiana State University Press, [2022] |
    Series: Southern messenger poets
Identifiers: LCCN 2021028658 (print) | LCCN 2021028659 (ebook) | ISBN
    978-0-8071-7620-7 (paperback) | ISBN 978-0-8071-7720-4 (pdf) | ISBN
    978-0-8071-7722-8 (epub)
Subjects: LCGFT: Poetry.
Classification: LCC PS3618.O456 S55 2022 (print) | LCC PS3618.O456
    (ebook) | DDC 811/.6—dc23
LC record available at https://lccn.loc.gov/2021028658
LC ebook record available at https://lccn.loc.gov/2021028659

for Rebecca,
again and always

&

for Callaway and Emmaline
and the other descendants of
the 7th Tennessee Volunteer Cavalry (USA)

Our vanity, our passions, our spirit of imitation, our abstract intelligence, our habits have long been at work, and it is the task of art to undo this work of theirs, making us travel back in the direction from which we have come to the depths where what has really existed lies unknown within us.

—PROUST

I'll always be poor in my mind.

—CHET ATKINS

Contents

Acknowledgments

Grateful acknowledgment is made to the editors of the following journals where some of these poems first saw the light of day: *32 Poems, Cumberland River Review, Gamut, Image, Our Jackson Home, The Missouri Review, Ploughshares,* and *The Southern Review.*

"Election Day Shooting at Middleburg, Tennessee, November 4, 1924, with Excerpts from the November 7 Edition of *The Lexington Progress* and Auburn Powers' *History of Henderson County*" has been anthologized in *Gracious: Poems from the 21st Century South.*

I am grateful for the support of a grant from the National Endowment for the Arts and a Witter Bynner Fellowship at the Library of Congress. Union University continues to sustain my work as a writer. Several of these poems got their start during residencies at the Virginia Center for the Creative Arts. And much thanks to Dave Smith: every word he said about this book made it better.

Shift Work

Fast Only Running Downhill

All they wanted to talk about was cars. Every one of the old guys ordering
    coffee at the City Café had driven something hot

in his misspent youth, maybe a repaint Chevelle barely street legal, raised
    letter tires all around, a four-fifty-four under the hood,

shaved heads and a carburetor kit. Now they were lucky if the frayed
    timing belt of a four-cylinder Civic got them to Walmart

and back. In the years I lived at home the only car we bought new was a
    Ford LTD Landau. My father had to explain to me

the formaldehyde stink of the carpet and the off-gassing of adhesives
    made a smell we were supposed to love. When I asked him

what LTD stood for, he knew the answer: "Long Term Debt." I could
    already recite "Fix Or Repair Daily" and "Found On Roadside

Dead." By the time I was old enough to drive, the note had been paid off,
    the vinyl roof was showing some age,

and if the car had a smell, it smelled of hard miles. The only thing new
    about it was a set of steel-belted radials. There's a long downgrade

out on New 22, a stretch of highway with no place for a trooper to hide.
    One night coming back from shooting pool two towns over

I decided to see what the old Ford would do. I stomped it to the floor as if
    I could kick the car downhill faster. The midnight's stillness

was without limit, and speed only fetched it nearer. The car had 120 mph
   on the clock, but down a road that was nothing but straightaway,

I couldn't bury the needle, which disappointed me even as the asphalt
   blurred to a watery smoothness under the headlamps,

the old engine redlined and uncomplaining. I would think back on that
   night, though, every time I needed to wring a little performance

out of whatever economy car we'd bought to make ourselves feel
   righteous—covering the 80 miles to the airport in 55 minutes

to fly to a bedside in Savannah, or driving like Steve McQueen all the way
   to Baptist Hospital before the baby came—how that old Ford

was built to run at its top end, downgrade or no downgrade, steady as a
   cruise ship at 110-miles-per, for as long as I kept the peddle down.

Stream Channelization

The water had it right, but our ideas ran contrary. In draining the Beech
    River bottom, crooked feeder streams got turned into ditches

as straight as the Army Corps of Engineers could dig them. To a farmer's
    eye, the regularized land looked like money. What good was anything

if you couldn't grow it in rows? Simplify, simplify. You can smell the
    resentment in the defeatured fields, the ground embarrassed

to be stripped of its hardwoods and still water, ridded of winter waterfowl,
    scarred by a ditch as inerasable as the crease in an old letter

set to fall apart from one more reading. It's wrong to be in love with such
    simplicity. Water wants to bend and meander. We were supposed to be

hunting, but my mind always wandered, thinking about how we believe we
    don't need to change but the land does, about how we've failed to honor

the water's wishes, how a straight line is the least lovely distance between
    two points. We tramped past a family grave plot so long undisturbed

it'd become a waist-high hillock risen from the eroded field, crowned with
    broom sage that moved when the wind moved and illegible tombstones
    that didn't.

In Memory of Calvin Purvis

The galvanized trashcan had to be picked up and carried to the curb if you
    didn't want it to leave a chalky scar scraped snakewise

down the driveway. The other men on the crew came and went, but Calvin
    Purvis held fast to the back of the garbage truck

year after year, lifting his gloved hand in salute to the neighborhood kids
    on ten-speeds and coaster bikes calling out,

"Hey Cal-vin!" in bright voices. We loved the hauler of our trash and
    needed him to have a name. Even with twice-a-week pickup

it was a one-garbage-truck town. Nobody'd heard of recycling. We didn't
    think much about trash except as a word

to throw around, useful to describe reading material that wasn't approved
    of, or people: any man sitting on a porch stoop

during business hours—if you could push a broom, why weren't you
    working a job?—or the brassy girls who showed up late

for high school, always a hickey on their neck, then disappeared with every
    intention of earning a diploma once the baby was born.

After a day on the truck, Calvin could be found at the city park watching
    his nephew play shortstop. With a hint of a stammer,

he'd yell, "Thow your high ball, kid!" no matter who was on the mound.
    He wouldn't sit in the bleachers and never let on

if he was surprised by what we'd decided to toss away. Who were we to
    complain if he wasn't particularly gentle with the trashcans

that rusted out before we got around to replacing them? They always came
    back empty enough and upright on the curb.

Now he's gone. We will all of us one day be as absent as the fast girls from
    first-period history class, unmissed as the discards

at the city dump, where teenagers park in winter, the dashboard light so
    low it's hard to judge the crest of need in each other's eye.

Election Day Shooting at Middleburg, Tennessee,
November 4, 1924, with Excerpts from the November 7
Edition of *The Lexington Progress* and Auburn Powers'
History of Henderson County

Hattie Lloyd Todd, aged eleven, saw them fall in the street—Tuke
    Bartholomew and his son Bud, the Democrats in charge

of the ballot box. In a few years she would be married to the nephew of the
    next man to die. He was W. W. Rogers, a Republican

and son of Tennessee Unionists, shot through the head when he tried to talk
    some sense to his friend Dan Powers,

who was wielding the gun that day of the national election and a fair
    marksman even when blind with rage. The assassin walked away

unpursued. Everyone in three counties traveled to Oak Grove Cemetery in
    such conveyances as were available, three fresh graves

spaded out of the clay, a year's worth of funerals on a single afternoon.
    Dan Powers hid out in the barns and corncribs of sympathizers

until he fled in the night, months of vagabondage taking him as far as
    Mexico and then Cuba before returning home to face a jury

of neighbors and distant kin. Not long into his life sentence, he took a razor
    to his throat, this killer of three people, one of them

his own good friend. There's not much burg to Middleburg anymore. The
    store burned down; the farms were foreclosed on. No call

to go back except to bury the dead. At the end of a long and fretful life
   Hattie Lloyd Todd Rogers was laid to rest while a blue jay scolded

from the upper limbs of a cemetery cedar. We always considered my
   grandmother to be as flighty as a songbird, touched by fears

and superstitions, and wouldn't have thought to ask what went through her
   head every time an engine backfired. Any dark cloud

reminded her of the tornado that spun their house down a hill and left it
   next to a splintered Spanish oak. I recalled asking her,

"Where'd you go?" She was defenseless against the memory. "We tacked
   up a little more tar paper," she said, "and went on living in it."

The Decline of Print Journalism

The paperboy must have been fifty years old, dragging a foot, afflicted
    with some kind of nervous disorder. He was always in need

of a shave. A thread of saliva wouldn't come unsewn from the whiskers of
    his chin. Since he had such trouble making change, fishing forever

in a filthy carpenter's apron to bring out any coin but the right one, we
    tried not to hand him folding money, which was in short supply

anyway. He worked the restaurants on Cumberland Avenue—The Torch,
    The Varsity—where we stumbled in before classes

and sat down to bacon and eggs-any-way, biscuits draped in milk gravy,
    and a side of grits, all of it next to a crisp city edition

of the Knoxville *News-Sentinel*. News still came on newsprint strapped in
    bundles and pushed off a truck before the sun came up.

I received it as a blessing when the paperboy pretended to recognize me.
    "They he is," he would say, and reach me a paper. All of us were certain

our talents would take us far. Did the paperboy like our chances? He
    visited each table in the row of banquettes and we tried to act

as though we would dwell in that college town forever, but the quickest
    glance told him we were short-lived as the soy ink

applied to 500 papers a minute at the presses down on Church Street, soon
    to rub a shadow on the fingers of a shrinking readership.

Outside, a coin machine held an untouched stack of the *New York Times*,
  expressed in from Atlanta if they hadn't been bumped

from the morning flight. The waitress couldn't help glaring at me as she
  tucked the check between the sugar and creamer, hoping

to turn the table before her shift was done. The busboy didn't lack for
  patience: to him every reader was just another plate to clear

as he wiped up the circles the water glass had stamped on the laminate
  tabletop and folded the wrinkled newsprint into the trash.

The College of Hard Knocks, Son

The school was still new the day I started first grade, flat-roofed
    modernism in a field of white clover, brown stains already blooming

in the ceiling tiles. It was built on the Stokes farm that hugged the edge of
    town. Every afternoon Old Man Stokes, his eyes unreadable

behind prescription sunglasses even on the cloudiest day, stood under his
    apple tree while the foot traffic passed like an invasive species

creeping along the nameless new street that accessed the school. We were
    being prepared for a future no one could foresee, our rough edges

knocked off, made polite and tractable. I hadn't stopped wanting to learn
    everything, so I always had a question for him. When I asked

if the green apples would ever be ready for picking, he said, "You don't
    want one of those," and looked at it as coldly as Jesus

looked at the fig tree, "A few might be worth putting in a pie but they're
    too sour for much else." The school board had taken his best acres,
    promising

city water and sewer lines to raise the value of the rest of his place, but as
    soon as the contractors broke ground his improvements got cut

from the budget. Mrs. Stokes, skeptical of all progress and the happier for
    it, dried the green apples on sections of galvanized metal roofing laid

across saw horses. Part of her day's entertainment was guessing what
    question I would have when I came walking by at 3:05. It seemed to me

the old farmer knew everything there was to know, so one day I asked him
    where he'd gone to college. My parents were schoolteachers—I thought

everyone had a degree or two on the wall. He laughed a laugh that sounded
    like it'd been saved up and allowed to draw interest, and said

in a voice his wife could hear all the way to where she was sorting apples,
    "The college of hard knocks, son!" I'd never seen him

so pleased. What was left of his land would still produce. Beans were
    bringing $3.79 a bushel and were planted right up to the edge

of school property. We couldn't keep our eyes on the worksheets we'd
    been given, damp and stinking from the mimeograph machine,

when a towering Massey Ferguson combine showed up to harvest them,
    trailing a slipstream of chaff and dust until the field was stripped clean

and its chute swung over the open box of a twelve-ton truck for the beans
    to come streaming out, uniform and golden in the late-season light.

Last Shift at the Slipper Mill

I knew where the shoes came from, boxed in pairs, swaddled in tissue
   paper wrinkled and white as bed linens, some laborer's labor

lingering in the folds. We practiced baseball on the diamond behind the
   shoe factory, and I could watch the tractor-trailer rigs

back up to the loading dock and leave out again laden with what my
   neighbors made. Mike Hayes, waiting to take his swings,

had been pegged with a foul ball—no surprise the red-stitched seams left a
   mark, but it was magical how you could read *Wilson*

on his arm as clearly as it was stamped on every ball in the bucket. Easy
   not to think about who sewed your Sunday shoes now

that they're floated here on Panamanian-flagged container ships from far-
   off countries where human labor costs next to nothing.

I don't know who makes the shoes these days, not personally, but I used to.
   I was taught to address them as *sir* and *ma'am,*

and played on ball teams with their kids. We sat beside each other in
   school, shared a pew on Sunday. It was impolite to ask

about someone's work. No one wanted to talk about a job like that, or the
   wages that went with it. Taking fly balls,

we couldn't pay much attention to the shift change, skeins of workers
   shambling through the double doors to find their cars

in the parking lot, not much chatter between them. Who wasn't being bent
   by their work like leather on a last? The baseballs

in the practice bucket were brown as the clay-colored clouds and hard to
   track when Glenn lofted them out to centerfield

with an easy swing of his bat. On the way home, if we met a second-shift
   worker at the four-way stop on Magnolia Street, my father

would lift two fingers from the steering wheel and elicit a polite nod in
   response so they could decide whose turn it was to go first.

Empty Storage Unit in Texas

It all went into storage when he gave up and came home—a rutted-out
    mattress and bed frame, the couch and love seat, boxes full

of mismatched dishes and the cheapest kitchen implements that would
    serve, a chrome-plated curl bar but no weights. He left a shearling coat

he wouldn't be needing for awhile, proof he wasn't gone for good. The
    color TV went back to the rent-to-own store, but somehow

he was stuck with the stand it came on. How many times did you have to
    pay for something before you could say it was yours? Dallas

was a boomtown, young people drawn there dense as butterflies weighing
    down the trees where they overwintered, sprawling

apartment complexes redolent of drywall mud and curing paint. It's
    embarrassing what you accumulate, such a pile of cheap, shiny things

soon to lose the shiny but never the cheap. He and his one acquaintance
    with a pickup loaded the unit full in a single afternoon,

hooked a new padlock through the hasp and walked away while it was still
    swinging. The primer on how to leave a town is in the fine print

of a storage unit contract. Back home he took a state job—health and
    dental, two weeks' vacation, a retirement plan—no time

to dwell on the day he quit Dallas and what'd been left behind, how the
    locker's echo was silenced by all he couldn't keep. He'd paid

the first three months in advance, and when his remittances were overdue,
   as per the latter clauses in the contract, not on the first day,

or the first month, but when they got around to it, when they had a renter
   for the unit, they sent a workman with bolt cutters, not even

curious about the contents, more junk to auction off, maybe some
   electronics to draw a bid, the rest of it bound for the landfill, freeing

a 5'×10' unit, swept out and reverberating, ready to accept all the worldly
   possessions you didn't know you were parting with forever.

Last Tenant in the White Farmhouse

She'd found a countrywoman to do her sewing. After supper she drove out
    an unlined road paved years ago but so much patched

it'd gone back to gravel. The railroad crossing sign wore a pattern of rusty
    stars from a load of #9 birdshot. Sheet lightning

was being pinned up over in the bootheel, pale and predictable. No great
    trick to assemble a history from the smells in the kitchen heat

escaping through the warped screen door, a savor of buttermilk souring in
    the biscuit dough, gun oil off a whetstone

to sharpen the butcher knife, the last Vidalia onion fried with the pork
    chops. This was the way people had always done: piecework

on top of small farming to bring in a little pocket money. Why couldn't
    they still live like that? Everybody she knew

had taken a town job where the porches on the just-built ranch houses, if
    they had porches, were shallow and useless. Off in the distance,

the lightning was beginning its own delicate stitchery. This would be the
    last handmade dress she'd ever wear. Hemlines had climbed

as high as they could go, and no-iron shirts were almost as good as their
    word. Men had forgotten how to wear hats. It would soon seem peculiar

for anyone who could get honest work to take the time to sit down and sew.
    The seamstress was already a ghost. From a TV set

in an upstairs room, Porter Wagner's half of a duet was a warning that
   something more final than the weather was coming to obliterate

the economy of this small plot, where the past had been emptied like the
   lidless Mason jars forgotten in the garden shed. The day was done

when your nicest things were made by hand, when a store-bought bolt of
   cloth carried up to a farmhouse door could come back

human-shaped and wearable—a complicated, womanly shape at that,
   conformed to a few measurements taken one stormy night and adjusted

to a pattern as rendible as cigarette paper, pinned on blue chiffon to be
   chalked and cut with shears the seamstress will never wear out.

Mourning Dove

There's a mourning dove outside on the power lines that won't shut up.
　　She's probably not mourning any-damn-thing, but only knows

the one song. I should give her more credit: you can chronicle the history
　　of heartache in the shaping of a five-note phrase. Technique is hard to see

when it's what's making you weep. The final attainment of the virtuoso is
　　learning to keep it to yourself. The ramshackle nests doves build

lack virtuosity, that's for sure, porous as my own house with its single-pane
　　sashes ninety years old admitting all the raucous birdsong and a good slice

of the wind. Greetings of passersby squeeze in with the drafts and far-off
　　train sounds. The street is black from last night's rain. Roof shingles shine

and pretend to be new. Before I realize it, the dove is done, but even the
　　silence gets in here to distract me while I'm trying to make something

with the words I know. How is it that all birdsong is happy save for one?
　　Just wait. She'll start up again, and I won't succeed at ignoring her,

constant mourner, world's worst nest builder, song-fashioner from five
　　frayed notes that can't be kept out of this leaky house.

Rubbernecker

He'd driven these roads so long that over every third rise he had a story to
    tell of a deadly wreck he'd witnessed. Back then

you got out and did what you could to help, directed traffic if you had to,
    until the Highway Patrol took charge. Once he watched

as motorists laid a man and woman on the porch of a crossroads store
    shoulder to shoulder. A passerby hesitated, but only a moment,

before he shed his windbreaker and gave them their privacy. The posted
    speed limit went largely unobserved, a broken line of paint

all that protected you from oncoming traffic. Saturday nights, people went
    to gaze at the wrecks on the highway. Weegee and Warhol

weren't the first rubberneckers to own that carnage contained the makings
    of art, out-of-control skids striking lovely arcs

across the macadam, the curved sheet metal of fenders and decklids
    become buckled and bent, windshields bursting outward,

assembly-line silhouettes now one of a kind. A 4"×6" guardrail beam from
    one of the wooden bridges in the Hatchie bottom

had punched a rectangle through the windshield of a new Studebaker. The
    driver's brains made a tidy pile in the back seat. Take care

what you turn your head to look at, he was learning, because it might exact
    a grain of effort every day to keep it forgotten. On US 412

out of Parsons, Tennessee, a family sedan was blocking both lanes, tires
    up, tempered glass strewn like shaved ice from a snow cone

too stubborn to melt. He joined a group gathering to right it so the wrecker
    could clear the roadway. Many hands make light work, even

when it's turning over an automobile. As they rolled the car, blood that
    had pooled in the roof streamed onto the asphalt

and was still shining in the glare of his headlights after he'd wiped his
    sticky loafers in the grass and gotten back behind the wheel.

Making Book

I hated Sunday shift. Time clung hard to every brick and tree limb in that
    Baptist town where there was still something sinful

about commerce on the Lord's Day. I had no use for a day of rest and took
    a job working retail at a tick above minimum, praying

the hours would move. Across the concourse, rows of lensless eyeglasses
    watched the optometrist on the phone all afternoon

taking last-minute bets. What else was there to do on a Sunday with no
    foot traffic? Blue laws kept the package stores closed,

and liquor by the drink was a decade away. The optometrist was one man
    when fitting tortoise shell frames for a customer, another

when he picked up the phone: he spoke a few words and wrote something
    down, and before the handset went back on the cradle

the words were a contract. We were all looking for tricks to make the time
    pass. Put a little money down, see if that helps. On the surface,

our neighbors seemed as simple as the optometrist-bookie's unwrinkled lab
    coat, as predictable as the mall's looped Muzak, so flavorless

you couldn't tell when it repeated. I could say to the penny what my time
    was worth when Becky handed me a paycheck on the fifteenth

and the thirty-first that would barely make rent. We walked the day's
    receipts to the depository as if something precious was hidden

in the bank bag. Money was supposed to make things matter, but all that
  has lasted is the damn music that never stopped and echoes

of footsteps in the after-hours mall, and maybe a character or two I've kept.
  My roommate had a C-note down on every NFL game, trying

to recoup his Saturday losses, and it could have been with this guy for all I
  knew. Collection day was coming, and he was already in too deep

to repay, sweating bullets over beating the spread, while the weekend
  dragged on for the rest of us unwilling to wager what was already spent.

Yellow Jacket Nest

The nest was buried beside the water meter in the front yard. They'd built
    so deep the yellow jackets must have felt

the hard winter half a year away. My son was cutting the grass when they
    swarmed him, a knot of wasps intent as any of God's creatures

on surviving through to the next season. I heard the power mower choke
    down and the boy's screams but didn't know

the cause of it until I rolled back his sock and one of the yellow jackets that
    boiled out stung me on the knuckle, an electric stab

as though I'd touched it to bare wire. So easy assigning motivations to the
    clouds and the wildlife, most every act

fitted with a reason, even cruelty explained away. I could see the wasps,
    angry as they ever are, elbowing out of the hole in the ground

and taking flight. They mark their enemy. If an insect can be said to have
    an idea, it's protect what's theirs. Do they feel any better

for the pain they've brought? I don't understand my own reasonings, but I
    knew the boy would have something to remember

from that year besides the record snow the yellow jackets predicted.
    There's a kernel of hate inside us that will burst and root

no matter the weather. The dented gas can was handy so I poured the nest
    hole full. "How about you light it?" he said, forgetting

his pain for a moment to see if I'd do it. "The gasoline's ruined that nest,
    son. No sense killing anything twice." It would be a long night

with the poison in his blood, running a low-grade fever, a swollen foot
    elevated on pillows, his face distorted into something not quite his own.

What if the cruelty of wasps wasn't cruelty at all? I settled him on the
    couch with ice on his ankle and a book he wouldn't feel like

opening, then I went back outside with a box of kitchen matches and for no
    reason dropped a lit one down the empty nest hole.

John Fergus Ryan Asks Politely for a
Second Helping of Bourbon Balls

That John Ryan had gifts as an artist and that he leaves behind a legacy of
literary achievement are both givens. Those who knew him, though, will most
remember him not primarily for his tropes but for his friendship. It is ironic
that Ryan liked to see himself characterized by his wry and often-quoted
aphorism "People are no damn good."
—Jackson Baker's obituary in the *Memphis Flyer*

We would never be famous ones for entertaining, but we've had our
   moments. Newly unpacked from the honeymoon, it was time

to throw a party for all the friends we couldn't afford to feed at our tiny
   wedding. I painted the public rooms of the bungalow

we were renting, and Rebecca set out vases of Queen Anne's lace and
   floated magnolia blossoms in salt glazed bowls. Then she began

to bake. Finger foods on fancy crackers, bacon-wrapped this and thats,
   hors d'oeuvres of every savory stripe. And those bourbon balls

from her grandmother's handwritten recipe card, rolled in confectioner's
   sugar—how much Maker's Mark darkened the measuring cup

would stay a family secret. Of course we invited him. John was from Little
   Rock and understood bourbon balls. He took breakfast in the same café

where I worked some mornings, trying to keep my draft pages out of the
   red-eye gravy inky with ham drippings. He had a couple of novels

still in print and was in less of a hurry, ready to chat until the humorless
   waitress quit warming his coffee. A good party's as ephemeral

as the short story he'd published in the *Evergreen Review* before it went
   belly up. We were about to start washing the dishes,

just a guest or two lingering, already congratulating ourselves on our first
   big do, when there was a tap at the front door

and John let himself in. The flames had burrowed deep into the pillar
   candles on the window sills. "Would there be any bourbon balls left?"

I peeled the foil from the platter and brought them to the coffee table—
   already leftovers, but some things are better that way—and we sat down

to talk about the books we venerated and the ones we didn't, and see if we
   could find forgiveness in our hearts for those big city writers

who got all the breaks, though John had long ago figured out the town we
   were living in was a plate that would never get emptied.

City Beautiful

In the large photographs they want $1,200 for, the lens found something to
 linger over in the building's decay, the old Sears Tower,

so long abandoned it became beautiful in its ruination, the walls mold-
 stenciled and textured with curls of lead paint, casement windows

clouded by neglect where they still held on to glass. Beauty is fragile, can
 we agree on that? Here and gone. There's something delicate

in a demolition site, twisted #8 rebar as pretty as a spray of plaited braids.
 Maybe every city is a construct made in the mind

but the toe of my boot keeps catching on the bucked-up sidewalk sections
 of this one. Disregard can be a technique of art, weeds greening

the cracks of the parking lot, broken windows composing a variation across
 the strict meter of a façade. Hard to compete with ruins

for beauty. In this town of tagged overpasses and stuttering streetlamps,
 potholes are distributed like eighth notes on a staff

along streets traveled by high-mileage sedans that wouldn't make it through
 inspection in another city, the occasional passenger-side window woven

from duct tape. Two cars pass, and there is something intimate in how
 closely one is following the other, a tow chain sparking

on the asphalt between them. Perhaps those sounds aren't gunfire at all, six
 pops and no siren ever answers. There's a map of gun crimes

updating on the city's website every seven minutes. You can buy magnetic
   decals of bullet holes to affix to your car and show a sense of humor

about the whole thing, but then you get out at a gas station and realize the
   bullet hole stickers on the car next to you aren't stickers at all

but empty bullet holes in the fender and door, coronaed with scab-red rust
   where the slug took the paint and clearcote with it. The driver

lights a cigarette under the No Smoking sign and doesn't startle when the
   tank fills and the pump chokes off. He's contemplating some vanishing thing

down Watkins Avenue and will finish whatever thought he's having before
   he pulls the nozzle from the tank and screws on the cap.

Valentine's Day Eve, Dinstuhl's Fine Candies, Memphis, Tennessee

I had come to the end of my formal schooling, my studies in history were a
    thing of the past. I was in history now, just another customer

at the crowded candy store, new to town, the chilly evening before
    Valentine's Day. We were packed tight as the heart-shaped boxes

we'd lined up to buy, empty of love and irritable at the wait. I was
    determined to live where I lived, at street level: there's no living

that doesn't take place in a place. I'd forgotten for a moment I was
    shopping for something sweet, something handmade and local

to give in gratitude. The man in front of me looked like he'd lived here
    forever, too old to go into the office but still dressed for it,

immaculate suit and cashmere topcoat, his hat in his hand. I'd been taught
    to predict the past, but he could tell you the present. It was this way

every year, and he would have been worried if it wasn't. His serenity was
    as formal as a hand-written thank you note addressed to the harried
    woman

who weighed out his orange rings, half-dipped in dark chocolate, then
    wrapped them in last year's pink paper gaudied with blood-red hearts.

How to Change a Flat

He ran his tires so thin you could see the air inside them. Any money left
over at the end of the month went into rebuilding

a burnt-out clutch, or installing glasspack mufflers to get that throaty note
he thought a car should have. You wanted slick tires

to peel out and smoke as you leapt off the line. He loved that flathead Ford,
but in a couple of years he'd be ashamed to see it parked

in the driveway. He could only guess what he would have to do to leave
this place the highway'd missed, but he hoped he already knew

how to do it. Coming home after a Friday night date, maybe with Laura
Leigh Crowder or Baby Girl Johnson, a tire went down

on an unlined piece of road. Dark out there in the country, but he didn't
need any light to get the jack set and break loose the lug nuts.

He could smell the storm that had been coming on since he'd walked his
date up to the door. He cranked on the jack handle to clear the wheel

then started spinning the wrench and dropping lug nuts into the hubcap. He
was leaving Decatur County just when he'd learned

every jukebox that would give you an extra play and all the shortcuts down
nameless gravel tracks. He could call the peace officers by name

and drove their daughters to the movie show, and had finally figured out
how much hip the pinball machines could stand. Summer was done

and the girls were going back to teachers college; he had a job waiting a
    hundred miles away on a City of Memphis surveying crew. What if

none of his skills would travel? The rain was making a marching sound up
    the road behind him. A bolt of lightning raked so close

it left a taste in the night. He yanked at the wheel and fitted on the spare,
    quick as a pit crew at Bristol Motor Speedway. The first thick drops

rang on the fender's sheet metal as he threaded the lug nuts blind and spun
    two of them tight. Two would hold at least as far as home.

Big Smith Brand Overalls, Stiff and New

They played dominoes on the porch of Tolley's Store, outfitted in bib
    overalls like they had a crop to finish, "Real go-getters,"

I heard someone say before we got out of the car, "—they'll drive their
    wife to work at the factory, and when her shift's over

they go get her." Machines had come to work the fields, so they sat on
    wooden soft drink cases and stirred the dominoes

pips-down before drawing the next hand. Wasn't this what crossroads
    stores were for? And it wasn't even a crossroads, just a bend

in not much of a road at all, kept paved by the county, no center line. They
    weren't sure what had reduced them to local color

but dispensed opinions about it just the same, dressed for the past in Big
    Smith overalls from the Co-Op, Hush Puppies oxfords

too worn to wear to church, an old felt fedora if it was after Labor Day and
    before Easter. Part of going home, my father visiting

with the men who were men when he was a boy, hearing the news of their
    children, whether they'd made a doctor or teacher

or just held on to steady work. They were proud of accomplishment. The
    economy was going to leave you behind, and the skills

your father'd taught you went out of style in a hurry. Though I wouldn't
    have believed it at the time, the polyester blend shirt,

polyester tie, and Sansabelt slacks my father ran the school in were just
   another uniform and would become every bit as dated

as what they'd worn to drag a picking sack down endless cotton rows
   from can see to can't. We could hear it before it got there,

a John Deere cotton picker come lumbering around the bend, the driver
   dressed in a polo shirt and polarized sunglasses

like he was on his way to get in a round of golf, an eight-track tape playing
   Glen Campbell songs behind the tinted glass of the cab.

He lifted a hand from the steering wheel, and they never failed to wave
   back, these men who, if you needed a piece of ground broke

with a two-mule plow, knew what it took and were wearing the right
   clothes to get up from their seat in the shade and have at it.

Flyover

The passenger jets were too high to hear, aimed at Chicago or Dallas,
    invisible save for a contrail drawn taut as a chalk line

until it got wiped off the sky by winds we couldn't taste from where we
    stood. No reason to lift your eyes, really. Nothing up there

had anything to do with a small town. If we drove to St. Louis there might
    be a flyover of F-4 Phantoms, low and dramatic

before first pitch, a tight finger-four formation meant to inspire, unbalanced
    yet perfect as a sonnet. Once at Busch Stadium

a live eagle was released during the national anthem. It flew a majestic
    spiral over the field, descending toward its handler

waiting at second base, then changed its mind and began another round—
    it was the Fourth of July, so we cheered the bird, and cheered

louder that it wanted to stay airborne, and a few of us booed when the bird
    finally settled on the handler's gauntleted arm to stab at

its reward. We were always being recruited to fill the ranks of the volunteer
    military. At the high school assembly, a Navy rock band

in service whites and spit-shined shoes played "Carry On My Wayward
    Son" before we were invited to have a word with the bass player

as we left the gym. Most of us weren't college material, but my parents
    were hopeful, dragging me to football games at Murray State

if the weather was nice. As we waited for kickoff, our attention was
　　directed to the dot of a helicopter in the afternoon sky,

just a short hop over from Fort Campbell, and five paratroopers flung
　　themselves out. I didn't even know I was living

in flyover country and was a little disappointed when the leader landed
　　on the 50-yard line and delivered the game ball to the official,

so graceful until his feet hit the artificial turf and he fought to collapse his
　　chute, which still had a mind to go wherever the wind was going.

Get Well Note for Elizabeth Caldwell

When my second grade teacher was dying, my mother had me sit down and
    write her a note. I was in the third grade by then

with no idea what to say. "Thank her for being a good teacher" (my mother
    was a master of the form), "and tell her you hope

she gets well soon." But I couldn't have said if she was a good teacher, and
    from the way it was discussed—not the words so much

as the perfection of the silences that shimmed them apart—the getting well
    soon was not in the offing. I'd already forgotten

most of second grade, which had been a repeat of first, nothing new to be
    learned except how to keep your pencil on the page

so a line of childish print could turn to cursive. Wasn't I supposed to leave
    it behind, get promoted and move on? She'd disappeared

into the house where her husband the doctor had already died. So I sat
    down finally and wrote the words I'd been told to write

in the slanting characters Mrs. Caldwell had taught me, but she was dead
    before the mailman delivered them, my get well note

staled into elegy. What's an elegy ever done for the elegized? It's a
    prettified excuse for not saying all you should have said

when it might have mattered. No town name was needed with the street
    address, just "City" and an 8¢ Willa Cather stamp. Why was it

this hard to get something down my mother could say so easily aloud?
   Every week on the way to piano lessons I rode my bike

past her house. The new owners would be working in the flowerbeds or
   washing their station wagon in the narrow driveway,

proud of their shelter. They'd scabbed on a layer of asphalt shingles and
   painted the bricks a stately gray, but the house never lost its name,

the Dr. Caldwell House, where my teacher died and a useless letter, penned
   in a creditable cursive hand, is waiting to be opened.

Unlicensed, Unbonded, Uninsured

If a tree needed to come down, the Vickers brothers were who to talk to.
  It's good to be the person who gets called

for something. They showed up in two trucks, one needed to jump off the
  other when it wouldn't crank. My father was paying

in cash money no one was going to report. My mother asked what were
  those Vickers boys' names again, and he told her: Unlicensed, Unbonded,

and Uninsured. I could see that not much more was required to become the
  expert in that town than to come when called. Already

a big wedge of the day had been wasted. "That whole crew smells like a
  whiskey still"—my father's voice could bring disgust and amusement

in the same breath. We watched the youngest brother rope himself into the
  post oak, and limbs began to fall, some large enough to gouge

shin-deep holes in the ground where they struck. The more shiftless
  brothers would amble over to start cutting them up

for cordwood, the other source of their untaxed earnings. My father liked
  talking to workmen, drunk or sober. There was a craft

to everything, he believed, and he wanted to hear about it. Everyone had a
  job to get right, some piece of expertise to contribute, even

if it seemed there wasn't much mystery to it at all. The brothers on the
  ground made half-hearted efforts to kick sawdust into the scars

their work left in the lawn. They were in the middle of a conversation
 that'd been going round and round for years, still able to laugh

at the same turns in the stories. Then they heard a flurry of cursing from
 above and the youngest Vickers came repelling

down the tree like an Army Ranger dropping out of a Huey, which he may
 have been not too long ago. His chainsaw had found

a beehive in a hollow member of the tree and the bees weren't taking it
 peaceably. The other Vickerses looked up in time to see

the limb twisting off with a baritone crack that echoed against the
 neighbors' houses. They skipped to the side so it could land

between them, a near catastrophe to be considered in silence, then they
 were all flailing and cussing, whirling like devil-possessed cloggers

until they found refuge in the cab of the closest truck, not caring if it was
 the one that wouldn't start. Miss Russelene Summers, retired

from the Home Ec. department at the high school, was who to call for bees.
 She arrived directly, donning her veiled hat and lighting

the burlap in her smoker. She located the queen and collected the workers
 to take home to her bee yard, but not before chatting with my father

about the clover crop as they brushed the occasional bee off their shirts.
 The Vickerses reemerged undiscouraged and got back at it, still

a lot of tree to cut down. "Bet they kept a bottle in the truck," my father
   would say, playing up their drinking a little more

every time the story got told. He knew enough not to burn the belt-high
   stump they would leave and kill the termites inside

who had their own work to be about. He could have stood out there all day
   watching the men finish a job which was becoming

a degree or two less dangerous with each cut, and would have, except his
   wife was in the doorway calling him to the phone.

Definition of Terms

I guess it's useful to know what the terms mean, but that's not all they
    have going on. Words have mass and shape; they burn

with a certain color flame when set alight; some conduct and resist and
    have a texture, a tooth, a hand and a drape. Words collect

blurry purple stamps from the frontiers they've crossed and get handed
    down and traded until they're forgotten, like an old 45

boxed in the garage. Pull one out. The Staple Singers, "Will the Circle Be
    Unbroken" on the Vee-Jay label, the grooves' abuse sighing

through the speakers just one more thing giving it soul. There's you a term
    that resists definition: what's it mean to have *soul*? Stax Records

on East McLemore, bulldozed in 1989, was rebuilt with bricks of regret,
    but the museum and school will never have soul the same way

as the repurposed movie house where Al Jackson, Jr.'s, drumwork and
    Duck Dunn's bass laid down a greasy beat so Big O's plaints

could soar and linger in the shadowy corners of that large room, reeled in
    through a Shure SM58 mic. In Memphis, just step outside

and soul is everywhere you turn. Breathe it in with the heat. It's the binding
    agent in a suspension of mosquitoes and jet engine moan.

It's what makes the sunlight adhere like a judgment to a hand-drawn Help
    Wanted sign and carries a report of gunfire to tap its signet ring

at the storm windows. No one owns the patent. Pops Staples' guitar playing
   has soul, strumming his Fender Stratocaster, and so does Mother Maybelle's,

scratching at her archtop Gibson on the Carter Family original. Anything
   that's sin-stained and striving can have soul. But you want

a definition that will obtain beyond South Memphis, don't you? How about
   this, then: Upriver there is a lovely thing, Saarinen's Gateway Arch,

a catenary curve. Any pure form comes with a calculus to graph it, but his
   drawings were dead and graceless, so Saarinen fabricated model after model,

eight feet tall, altering each one slightly, appraising it from every angle, in
   all kinds of light, until the arch quickened and sang. The distortion

in Saarinen's design, that's where the soul is—in the bending and
   compromising to make a curve too beautiful for any equation to describe.

In the Attic

The sound the pull-down stairs made was a chorus trying to tell the truth
    about the past, one shrill word—*Here*—screeched

in the soundbox of the attic. My mother hated to be up there by herself so
    she let me make the climb with her, each step creaking

even under a kindergartner's weight. Normally, I wasn't allowed to do
    anything halfway this adventurous. Between the queen posts,

the tongue-and-groove decking was stacked with cartons of belongings we
    hadn't figured out how to part with, the leftovers

of earlier lives, a library of clothbound textbooks from my father's time as
    a history major, dust jackets made of dust, pieces

of Bermuda green Samsonite packed with out-of-season clothes like they
    had train tickets for better weather, a bare bulb throwing

rusty light over the lot of it. Neighborhood sounds filtered in at the gable
    vents, julienned and weightless as confetti: I knew the names

that went with the voices and could tell you the color of the cars laboring to
    start. A rectangle of the familiar world was framed

in the opening we'd climbed through, side tables lemon oiled and doily
    topped, the living room rug mottled with curving

rows raked by the vacuum cleaner. No one'd told me there was a backstage
    and underside to everything where you could see

how it was joined together and might be pulled apart again. There was
    more storage in that attic than we had use for, but it took work

to save the possessions we couldn't bear to lose. I knew that when you lost
    something it usually stayed that way. Sometimes it was lost

when you kept it, even after being hauled up these steps, out of sight and
    out of mind above the ceiled rooms. I watched her open

a shiny box and take out a formal dress folded in tissue. She held it to her
    shoulders then refolded it, careful to move the creases.

Hunger

When it got so neither of them could be trusted with the stove, there was
    nothing for it but to be put in a home. At least

they'd be fed. His wife of sixty-two years dozed all day in a broken-down
    recliner they'd brought with them and hadn't said a word

that made sense in a year and a half. Jimmy the nurse's aid cut up her fish
    sticks then held a glass of milk while she took

mistrustful pulls at the straw. Saturday afternoons late his grandsons might
    stop by, the rankness of their hunting clothes

and whatever they'd stepped in undifferentiable from the nursing home
    smells. He liked hearing their adventures no matter

how luckless the hunt had been and knew the stories would have to satisfy
    him until the next visit. Since the throat cancer,

they retold his hunting stories for him, which they had by heart, all set
    during the Great Depression, how walking home once

from a job driving a team of mules for the Tennessee Valley Authority,
    saw-toothed shadows devouring another inch of ground

with every step he took, he'd eyed a wad of quail coveying up for the night
    in a patch of broom sage. He'd been trying to enjoy

his next-to-last cigarette of the day because there wouldn't be much supper
    behind it. When he walked in, he found a 12-gauge shell

in the bottom of the chifforobe and loaded it into his scattergun's left
  barrel. His wife asked him, "Now what?" and he said he'd be back

with meat for the skillet. No room for sport when your stomach's that
  empty. Shoot them on the roost. The boys couldn't get enough

of the one about the only other quail he'd ever killed. He was going out to
  cut wood and stepped into a covey—the explosion of birds

thrashing skyward startled him into swinging the axe off his shoulder with
  such surprise that he chopped a bird out of the air. A little something

to flavor the dumplings. After he'd worked until there wasn't one
  voiceable desire in his body beyond hunger, just about anything

could be called supper. Yesterday's cornbread crumbled into the
  buttermilk. Turnips boiled until they would chew. It compared favorably

to Ensure drained from a bottle or the applesauce and yogurt he needed
  Jimmy's help to get free of the packaging. In the evenings sometimes

a pair of quail emerged from the bean field to forage in the open, ready to
  take wing if any danger came close. He kept his chair

by the window to watch for them but wouldn't glance out until his
  grandsons were gone. He wanted to see if the birds made it through

till spring. A hawk was usually resting in a lightning-struck tree. The boys would soon finish their story and say it was time

to get their own supper, speaking as though the hunger they felt after a walk in the fields was something worthy of the name.

Crape Myrtle Pruning Guide

Be ready to regret everything. Every yank of the saw, every lop of the
  loppers. The crape myrtles are so acclimated to our conditions

it's hard to call them exotic. Just like us, they get by by forgetting where
  they came from. Stout enough for a child's climbing tree, they drink up

the drought and knit fists of crepey blossoms to swing like paper lanterns
  from arcing branch ends—panicles of lavender and icy white tempering

the summer's sear, ornaments for the old-fashioned dooryards. Their
  shadows fork like schematic diagrams of an ancient fireworks display.
  It's a trick

to prune them right. The gardening books warn you away from committing
  crape murder, but how could we resist taking off

a few of the lower branches to get a look at the complicated figuring of
  their cinnamon-red bark? They'll make plenty of new wood

without having to repair themselves from harsh treatment. We set out two
  Natchez crape myrtles beside our daughter's playhouse, miniature trees

for a miniature abode, and watched them grow as fast as the girl did. And
  they didn't stop, even after she never played there again.

To Evel Knievel, Jackie Fargo, and Bearcat Brown in Heaven
(with Their Complete Wardrobes)

I was never allowed to have a motorcycle or hang out with the cool kids
    who did, but nothing could save me from idolizing

Evel Knievel, who put his body at hazard jumping a stock Harley Davidson
    over cars and buses—15, or 21, or 23—always

a world-record attempt. I taught myself to ride wheelies on a hand-me-
    down coaster bike and took my turn jumping a 55-gallon barrel

until one of us broke an arm. We knew why crowds paid money to see a
    man dressed like a cross between Elvis Presley and Wonder Woman

perhaps not fail. It was as vulgar as the Saturday morning wrestling
    broadcast out of Memphis we couldn't stop watching, Jackie Fargo

in spangled tights getting the worst of it from some heel, Jackie reaching
    for his tag team partner Bearcat Brown, their fingertips

an inch apart. Every day we sorted the fake from the real but dreamed of
    launching ourselves like Jackie Fargo flying off the top rope.

We were as starved for attention as Evel Knievel when he rode to the top
    of the ramp to survey the distance he would jump, as needy

as the wrestlers in their ridiculous costumes going to fat, putting on a show
    in half-empty National Guard armories, sweating out

an athlete's diet of Porterhouse steak and frosted steins of Michelob. For
    Evel Knievel the risks were real. A hell of a thing

to put yourself through just to get your face on a Wheaties box. No such
   bargain would be offered to us, but we readied ourselves

in case it turned out we were somebody's hero, caught up in a life as
   untethered as Evel Knievel's motorcycle, a road machine

with no road beneath it, given flight for a moment, the rear wheel reaching
   for earth, then the shock of the front tire landing,

the rider flung over the handlebars, his delicate gloved hands reaching
   groundward to touch what was rising up so fast.

Ghost Map of Carroll County

We could always come up with a reason why a place was haunted. Every
    old house tried to be, and would call to you

in the least wind, restless spirits speaking their piece long after the last
    tenant left. Our spirits were restless, too. School was out

for summer, so we took to the back roads where the cicadas' operatic
    shrilling rose above the lower register accompaniment

of tires on gravel. We looked fearless in our newly issued driver's license
    photos. Before leaving the main road, someone'd flung

the last empty at a DO NOT PASS sign just to hear it shatter. In the dark
    corners of the county, you might come across

an abandoned house blacking a chord of sky, maybe the farmhouse where
    the dressmaker's stillborn twins had been heard

singing on the sideporch, children now, mournful and on pitch. We'd
    laughed at the ghost stories that were supposed to keep us

in line: Raw Eyes and Bloody Bones coming to snatch the bad kids; you'd
    be lost forever if you followed the swamp lights

into the dark. We would have chased any light at all as far as it would take
    us, there were so few lengths we wouldn't go to

to be scared. We went parking with our dates in the nameless cemetery off
    of Como Road, the rows of tombstones littered

with low-mileage condoms and flattened cans of Busch Bavarian beer.
   Who could say what was beyond the sweep

of the headlamps? It was dark out there where the legends were written. A
   half a dozen miles over the hill, the town murmured

its beckoning glow into a sky impatient for the first quarter moon to rise,
   but we turned our backs and let the stars swallow us

whole. Are you really alive if you don't fear being not alive? When
   something scared us enough we would turn it to story

and hand it around until we'd worn off most of the terror and all the
   wisdom, but, whether we could see them or not, the ghosts

weren't going away. Anything could be haunted. Like the hill where Isaiah
   Highsmith, drag racing just to show off—only pride,

no pink slip on the line—lost control of his 442 Olds, then lost an arm in
   the crash and his girlfriend lost her life. Or the stretch of road

down which Lennie Giddens raced the midnight train to the crossing in
   the Jarrel Bottom and won, but not by enough to matter.

For Mrs. Marilyn Smothers, Grading My Freshman
Essay on Adrienne Rich's Poem "Living in Sin"

She didn't give us many topics to choose from. I hauled around a textbook
    thick with voices I'd never heard—Donald Barthelme's

"The Sandman," Virginia Woolf lamenting what became of Shakespeare's
    sister, six lines from Lewis Simpson called "American Poetry"

which may have been just that. I loved best what went unassigned, every
    selection a strange new song. Was it music at all

humming from the f-holes of my life? Until then, the new voices I
    collected had to be gathered in by the radio. If the weather was right

you could pick up WLS out of Chicago. On the Memphis stations,
    Al Green was so tired of being alone. Tanya Tucker in heavy rotation

up and down the dial. The tuning made a different song—note and grace
    note, patch of static, then another note. I was living

by myself at the top of a flight of stairs, typing whatever ideas came to me
    onto sheets of cheap bond, a bottle of Wite-Out handy

to touch up my mistakes. Each daub left a blot whiter than the page. The
    stair treads writhed, just like in the poem

whose meaning I was trying to lay hold of, but no one in the apartment
    house said a word about my comings and goings

or the typewriter's late racket, each keystrike a difficult decision to undo.
Mrs. Smothers, home from Sunday worship, sat down

to try not to fall too far behind with her grading. The sermon, like all the
others, had been on sin. We are assigned a life—

maybe it's to teach out a career at a Baptist college. Her idea of grading on
a curve was to put on a record so the student writing might become

less painful to read, maybe Maria Callas singing highlights from *Tosca* or
the original cast recording of *West Side Story.* When my paper rose

to the top of the stack, the pages strung with pearls of typos, she wrote a
terse rebuttal for every point I'd hazarded, but still gave the thing

an A, probably because everyone else in the class had written on "The
Horse Dealer's Daughter." There was so much to read

and so many ways to read it: we were all anthologies getting thicker by the
day as we slowly learned to listen. I adjusted the FM antenna

tacked to the wall of my room. A single note's coloring was all it took for
me to recognize any George Jones song or the backing vocals

to "Jolene"—so many singers out there, voices I'd yet to hear, on stations
I couldn't pick up, maybe something out of Athens, Georgia.

Christmas Card from Kentucky

They wished they could take their friends with them when they moved. It
    wasn't far, trading one small town for another, not even

a hundred miles across the state line. A point of pride to keep in touch,
    long-distance calls on Sundays after supper, person-to-person

for Carleen to catch them up on the local gossip that wasn't local anymore,
    then Croft might come on the line with a hunting story

in or out of season—these were men who liked to laugh out loud—maybe
    that time in the ice storm, sleet freezing to their clothes

but the dog didn't want to quit so they kept at it, and when they got back to
    the house their ice-shellacked hunting coats stood up

as if phantom hunters were still in them. "Wasn't any weather bad
    enough," Croft said, "—long as we had birds." They could count on

a Christmas card with a Currier and Ives scene and a note penned inside,
    all the sentences happy with double underlinings

and exclamation points, except when she told them old Sport had to be put
    to sleep and Croft hadn't set foot in the field since.

It doesn't take much of a missive to bring a close friend close. Croft had
    someone send word when Carleen's cancer came back. Already

the day of the service before they heard she was gone, too late to get
    dressed, gas up the car, and make the trip. With no Carleen to write it,

they went a year without a Christmas card from the old town, and another,
    then it seemed like the holiday stamp on every piece

of December mail was canceled by a Kentucky postmark, season's
    greetings they wouldn't display on the mantel. No one was sure

of all the facts. Croft had wandered into the stubbled fields, winter again in
    the Ohio Valley, and was found before he was missed,

frozen to death, not even wearing a windbreaker, his cheek pillowed on
    a furrow edge trimmed with a selvage of linen-white frost.

Fortune Teller

In the dead of the evening, before we had to lock up the bookstore, she
    produced a tarot pack from her embroidered purse

as though it had something to prove. My scorn for occult mumbo jumbo
    may have seemed total, but not every variety of lying

offended me. Just because I thought something was horseshit didn't mean
    I couldn't want it to go on forever. We hadn't lost much

if we lost this job, so why not a card reading on company time? She
    claimed gypsy blood. I wasn't about to believe it, no matter

how many bracelets jangled at her wrist. She'd gone to high school across
    town and had a soft spot for the novels of Lawrence Durrell. The cards

were difficult to shuffle, too large to bridge, but her fingers were graceful
    as she handled them and came alive for the dealing out

of my fate. I knew to pay attention. This was the only gratis card reading
    a flinty-hearted doubter like myself was ever going to get.

I've forgotten what she turned over—the Fool, the Wheel of Fortune, the
    Tower, Temperance—did it matter? I had no part

other than the watching, and deciding whether or not to believe, as though
    the truth was a choice waiting to get made. My skepticism

was too polluted with superstition to be any kind of critique—I've never
    told anyone what she said the cards said for fear

they knew what they were talking about, laid down in rows beside the cash
register. It was Friday night and I had people to meet, an hour yet

before Tav Falco and Panther Burns hit at the Antenna Club. When I
stepped into the parking lot, the outcome of the evening

was foretold in the night air, which I'd believed to be empty of everything
except shadow, but was inscribed from margin to margin

with divinatory smells risen from rutted asphalt, and auguries whispered in
castoff traffic sounds stacked too deep to prize apart and name.

December

Miss Brawner's porch light burned all night long, but we never saw a
    visitor walk up to the door. My mother was protective

of our elderly neighbors. They were hers to care for and keep happy: Miss
    Brawner, Mrs. Alley, and Mr. Dunwoody living all alone

and forgotten. At Christmastime we brought them baked goods—nothing
    I was jealous to eat. The Bundt cakes were whitened

with confectioner's sugar as flavorless as drywall dust, and I couldn't
    understand what was to be gained by putting a piece of fruitcake

in your mouth. If she was trying to teach me charity, maybe this was how
    it looked, raw December weather, brittle tree limbs

hardly registering the wind's fits and starts, last year's coat snug on me as
    a straightjacket, not having much luck keeping out the cold.

Miss Brawner was a small creature with small hands, but one was much
    smaller than the other. Before I knew I was looking at it

she started telling me how, as an infant, she crawled into the hearth and by
    the time they'd hitched the team and made it to town

her fingertips were blackened and bursting. The doctor pruned them back
    to the first knuckle. She fanned her fingernail-less fingers

to prove it'd happened. My mother frowned as we walked up the hill to
    where Mr. Dunwoody lived. She was still put out with me

for noticing, but noticing was all I was good at. There was something in
the old people's stories they had a hard time getting

across. They could tell I was determined to hear it. Mr. Dunwoody's house
was the biggest house on the street, long a stranger

to a coat of paint, with a second story that hadn't been inhabited in years.
Time had made him so shrunken and bent that Miss Brawner's hand

would have fit perfectly at the end of his arm. He wasn't sure what to make
of my mother's visit, but he had some sweets to offer

in return. "You know what we used to call these chocolate drops?" he said,
holding out a chipped bowl made of jadeite Depression glass.

I did know, and knew I wasn't going to say it. The wind had lain and the
air faithfully imaged every sound, but the only sounds to hear

were our footsteps, not quite in time, as we walked down the hill home,
the closed curtains in the windows of our rental house now pinked

with lamplight. We were soon to move away, and there would be one less
visit for the elderly shut-ins whose names I can call for you still.

Road Game

The All-Star team's windy ride to Clarksburg, ten boys in baseball
uniforms clowning in the bed of a Chevy Silverado, sixty miles an hour

down Highway 22. Nobody's parents thought twice about it. That was
how you did things then—seatbelts were an infringement

of personal liberty. The truck was new and may have been driven with an
extra splinter of caution, but a blowout would have strewn ballplayers

half a mile down the roadway. I was a centerfielder who played too deep,
and probably haven't become any better of a parent,

but I've never let my own kids ride in the back of a pickup with their
rowdy teammates, not knowing to hope for the best, or even

that hope was called for. There's a ledger kept somewhere of all the
highway wrecks that never happened, a precise accounting

of dodged tragedy. I don't need to see how many times my name is in it.
We drove through a summer shower that day. If you were close

to the cab not a drop would touch you, but each of us took pains to show
the oncoming cars we didn't mind it no matter how much we got rained on.

Shift Work

The day the Salant & Salant shirt factory started to hire, it was time to give
    up tenant farming and move to town. All it took

was an hourly wage and the prospect of indoor work, Lloyd sewing
    through a ten-hour shift, Bit on the loading dock delivering

cut pieces in bound lots so the women at the machines could make
    production. Happy to have a paycheck, they weren't studying

no damn union, leaning on luck like always, and the providence of a
    distractible God. Decades yet before the machines were unbolted

from the factory floor and trucked off to Mexico. In the spring of 1938,
    Decatur County, Tennessee, *was* Mexico. The back

of Bitty's neck would stay crosshatched with deep creases from years spent
    all day bent over in the sun filling a twelve-foot cotton sack

with pinch-sized bolls. When you trade one exploitive system for another,
    it feels like a gift if the new one is slightly less so. They built

a room onto their tiny house in town, a place to lay by the old life—the
    iron bedstead, a chifforobe full of nine-patch quilts fringed

with dry rot, the wick in the coal oil lamp just as dry and ragged. They only
    walked in there to set something down and leave it

on the room's raw floorboards. No throwing anything away because what
    if a Greater Depression was gathering? They never forgot

where they came from, and brought home remnant fabric torn in strips to
   tie the tomato vines to the stakes. A town backyard had ground enough

for a few rows of peas and corn and yellow squash, something to put up
   against the winter. Their work was purer than the cloudy water

hauled from the well before they'd had a city tap to turn on. You would
   never get paid what your work was worth, but what else

was the day good for, dawn nudging the darkness over to Arkansas,
   coffee coming to a boil, hardly time to taste it before the next shift began.

The Shadow of the Gardener

Everybody admired Jim's garden. Retired and a long time widowed, he
    had all day to devote to it, laying out perfect rows

of corn and sweet bell peppers, yellow squash in sculpted hills, peas and
    butterbeans, the drooping limbs of hybrid tomatoes

that stayed beautiful long after they were picked, all of it planted on the
    TVA right-of-way behind our houses, the matched curves

of the high-tension lines deepening their arcs as the summer held on. He
    was a man precise in his habits, every morning noting

the conditions in his desk calendar, a pair of dusty engineer's boots always
    waiting by the back door. The word'd been passed

he wasn't interested in going through another round of treatments, but no
    one was surprised he planted a garden anyway

with his last draft of strength. It was the planting he loved most. Harvest
    was always a gamble, but he could count on us

hanging around if there were eggplants to be taken home, still sunwarm
    when we sliced and sautéed them. The doctors had said

weeks, not months. With Jim housebound the produce wasn't so bountiful.
    Somebody could quote, "The shadow of the gardener

is the best fertilizer," but Jim's ideas about fertilizers were less
    philosophical. So we weeded and we hoed, and during the dry spell

finally thought to drag a hose down there and irrigate. On his last day, a
  neighbor took the ripest Betterboys up to the house

for the hospice nurse to slice and salt for him. Ears of corn were ready to
  pull when we came home from the funeral, but they'd be overripe

and weevilly before any of us could bring ourselves to do it. The purple
  hull peas rattled in the pod and stained our hands blue as a bruise

after we'd shelled them. When it turned cold there were turnip greens to
  gather that didn't look like a crop at all but would feed you

just the same, simmered in fat, a little vinegar poured on top. Now, you
  have to know where it was to be able to see the once-cultivated plot—

the power lines still run straight from the coal-fired plant at New
  Johnsonville, but briars have come to reclaim that half-acre, chest high

and spiked with barbs that slash the dim silhouettes of blackbirds when a
  swarm of them rolls overhead in December's daylong gray.

Highway Song

Nothing to do with time but kill it. That town had no use for us. Who was
    it gave a damn if we came or went? Before school,

you could find Biggy and Birdman and Coz and Toombs outside the Kwik
    Stop finishing a breakfast of powdered doughnuts washed down

with swigs of Chocolate Soldier from a return-for-deposit bottle. Still a few
    minutes till second bell so why not take a ride

into the country? A band named Blackfoot was wailing the highway song
    we all liked out of someone's aftermarket tape deck hung

on brackets beneath the dashboard. Another day late to class just to hear a
    guitar jam finish. The teachers marking them tardy were done trying

to believe the future was unwritten for those who couldn't solve for x or
    come up with the next statement in the proof. We passed the time

getting in fistfights, crossing the street to settle our disputes off school
    property. Nobody'd told us that the art was in the knowing

how to slip a punch. All would be forgotten by the time the sun went down
    on Friday and the party got going, most of the senior class

standing around a keg set up beside an old barn listing eastward from so
    lengthy a career holding off the weather. This far from town

the 10:20 freight was already back up to speed, its approach sounding a
    little like Shorty Medlocke's harmonica intro to "Train, Train"

even when the dragging tape flattened the notes. A security light bolted
   above the empty barn's double doors went about its business

luring a congregation of insects for the evening bats to hunt. If you threw
   a rock at them, the bats swerved clear every time. It was a miracle

to watch, how they could tell what was coming at them out of the dark as
   surely as we knew the next word in every Lynyrd Skynyrd song, the bend

of every guitar lick from first note to fade-out. Here's how this song
   finishes: with boys throwing rocks at bats until the keg floats in the ice.

Rabbit's Foot

Mr. Brooks had to lean on a cane to get anywhere but always kept a project
  going in his shed. I was a boy of unknown promise

wearing leather-soled correction shoes—by my own lights, unlucky in all
  things. When I asked what it would take to get a rabbit's foot,

my father sent me to see the old man. Bob Brooks had walked the bottom
  of Carroll Lake before it was a lake and could recall a time

when no road in Carroll County had been muddied by the inflatable tires of
  an automobile. The secrets of the woods were as orderly in his mind

as the tools hanging on every foot of shop wall, grease black, each of them,
  and honed bright where their edges met with work. "It's better luck," he said,

"if you catch your own," and found some scrap boards to build a rabbit
  gum. He showed me how to guide the saw with my knuckle

to get it started in the kerf. Rough carpentry, but it would do to catch a
  rabbit. I found a game trail in the woods and baited the trap

with a wedge of sweet potato. Just my luck I'd been set down in a place
  with fields and woods at the end of every view, rabbits' feet

there for the taking. Luck was complicated. The left hind foot was where
  the luck was. Best if it came off a rabbit bagged

in a graveyard under a full moon on the grave-swell of the meanest son of
  a bitch in the place. Mr. Brooks never told me

what to do with the rabbit when I caught it. Let it go with all its feet
attached was my plan. On the morning the bait was gone,

a shower of sleet had frozen the trap open. I was glad. My shoes were wet
with frost from the woods when I took my seat

in Mrs. Caldwell's class to learn the difference between declarative and
interrogative. There wasn't much changing where luck landed.

Didn't it get passed down like General Motors shares? Whatever portion
was coming to me had already been arranged.

When rabbit season was over, I brought the trap in. Neither of us was
going to break any game laws. Let the rabbits

keep their luck. Mr. Brooks dug up a rabbit's foot from somewhere. "See
if there's some luck left in this one." It had lost a lot of its fur, just

a fortuneless gray claw on a cheap fob chain. I put it in my pocket and
waited for my luck to turn, and—who knows?—maybe it did.

Research

Christina had a gift for impressions. She came back from her summer job
    with a head full of voices. There was factory work

still to be had, a place on the production line next to the lifers. The money
    kept her in thrift store outfits and feminist theory

course texts. Research for her art, she called it, though she couldn't have
    said right then what her art would be. She was the first of us

to figure out that every homely thing was ripe to be transformed if you
    knew how to look at it. On smoke break at the factory

they'd learned Virgie was having a birthday. "It's just another day," Virgie
    told them, "just another *got*damn day." Christina

did the impression, complete with a pretend Winston filter-tip in her
    gesturing hand, and it was so successful the words became

our response for everything. When asked how the Econ exam went, we had
    Virgie's answer to give. There was a beer joint in Maryville

where Christina took us on her researches, Schlitz on tap and a long
    counter to sit at and consider your plate lunch. The food was inedible

but that wasn't what she was after. She wrote "Let's have us another *Slitz*,
    Ray" in her notebook as soon as it was said

by a hopeless case on a barstool drinking up a disability check and
    demanding to be heard. Her student apartment was haunted

with department store mannequins and other bits of scavenged décor
   arranged like the set design of some experimental play. Half-finished

canvases from her semester as an art major—large ones she'd wanted to
   look like discarded drafts of a Franz Kline painting—leaned

against the walls. So much work put into something with just a few weeks
   left on the lease. When she landed a role

in a student production of *Come Back to the Five and Dime, Jimmy Dean,
   Jimmy Dean*, we showed up to support her, sitting down front on
   opening night.

Weeks of rehearsal for five performances—six, if you count dress. It takes
   art to sound like what you sound like. The gleanings

from her field studies seasoned the notes of her voice, and if one colorful
   phrase got remembered, you couldn't call it just another day.

Laundromat Ashtrays in Charlottesville

Everybody looks alike on laundry day, I don't care what's been inked on
  your neck or how you've dyed your hair, down to your last clean shirt,

hollow-eyed and homesick, indistinguishable as the pale blue dryer sheets
  twisted in the trash. Our grammars were so scrubbed of nonstandard usages

we'd stopped sounding like where we came from. Whoever got paid to
  empty the ashtrays had lain down on the job. Every now and then

in that college town laundromat someone was smoking the right brand to
  remind me of back home, a soft pack of unfiltered Camels

square in my grandfather's shirt pocket, the one colorfast pleasure in his
  long laborer's day. He came trailing Turkish tobacco smoke and a cough

that sounded like it was made by a rusty ripsaw with a score to settle.
  Maybe we all had memories that needed to be stubbed out

in an overflowing ashtray before we could finish folding our whites and
  get back to the bookish pursuits we tried to call work. Would my people

know me when I got home? I bought a pack of Camels from the service
  station next door and sat on the curb to light one up, killing a few minutes

before I had to go back inside and throw my knotted laundry in the drum
  of a commercial dryer, still hot from tumbling someone else's clothes.

Unstructured Play after the Funeral

By the sound of it, you'd never know anyone was dead. Or maybe you
   would: in the way the kids' laughter and taunts refused to blend

with the other city sounds and rode like cream cheese frosting on all the
   bruitings we've learned to ignore, overdressed children

sent to play in the front yard, Texas cousins and the cousins down from
   Louisville joining in. They'd been sitting still long enough

at the church and then through the interment where they'd been quick to
   figure out that what was mounded beneath blankets of Astroturf

would shortly be shoveled back into the open grave. They kicked their
   shoes into a pile on the driveway, the boys losing their neckties,

shirttails flying free. The front door swung open and they all quietened
   down for a moment. Inside was where the mourners were

and they wanted none of that, the counter space in the kitchen taken up
   with casserole dishes full of food they didn't like

or even understand, all that brittle talk about times they hadn't been alive
   to live. An underinflated soccer ball was rolled amongst them,

and as soon as the door was shut, it was chaos again, the soccer ball
   becoming a dodgeball, then a baseball to some kid

fisting it with a left-handed swing. The girl from the travel soccer squad
   made them all look bad no matter the sport. They were done

with solemnity and quiet. Their hollering and name-calling could drown
out the ambulances slaloming through traffic to the Med

and the jet-whine of FedEx planes peeling themselves from a flypaper sky,
the afternoon air bright as new copper and just as fine

a conductor. The grownups were distracted but wouldn't have had the heart
to rein them in even if they were paying attention. It was the sound

of life, and became more alive as the play grew rougher, grass stains and
skinned knees, some unnamed game where whoever got their hands

on the ball took it and ran until chased down and tackled, the rest of them
piling on, not much difference between the cries of joy

from the top of the scrum of children and what was heard from those
pinned below, buried, but safely on this side of the sweet-smelling sod.

Andersonville Memento

When his third mount was shot from under him, my great-great-grandfather
  hopped on a tree stump, waved his saber and yelled, "Shoot this

out from under me, you rebel sons of bitches!" Hard to tell how true the
  family stories were. That one sounded like it came standard issue

with every trooper's discharge papers. He and his brothers enlisted on the
  same afternoon—the 7th Tennessee Volunteer Cavalry, USA not CSA—

Tennessee Unionists out of the poor river counties, and didn't see each
  other again until the stockade of Andersonville Prison. It was said

they'd befriended a feist dog and slaughtered it just to stay alive. Not every
  memory could be wreathed in honor. The last time

they were surrendered, Nathan Bedford Forrest broke his worthless word
  and took their money and boots, all their equipment, and transported them

south. In the histories penned by glorifiers of the Lost Cause it might be
  worth a couple of sentences, how the Union garrison

was shown cannon made of fallen logs and duped into laying down their
  arms. No mention of the violated terms of surrender or the forced march

to an open stockade in Georgia to starve. Storytelling is never done. Some
  are hard to make polished and artful, like the one

where he was separated from his unit, no mount, the rain starting to freeze
  and night coming on. He'd fared better than his horse,

but he was shot through the neck, lost and wet. Time to lie down and die,
    he reckoned, when he rousted a drove of wild hogs

out of a hollow tree, as good a place as any to give up, so he crawled in
    and shivered until shivering didn't interest him anymore

in the bitter cold. But then the swine returned and crowded around him. He
    would swear it was the animals' foul breath and not their body heat

saving him that night—one more story to circulate, like the leg bone of the
    dog that kept them from starving, passed from family to family.

Notes

BOOK EPIGRAPHS
The Proust selection is from *In Search of Lost Time, Vol. VI: Time Regained,* trans. by Andreas
Mayor and Terence Kilmartin, p. 300, revised by D. J. Enright.

Chet Atkins (1924–2001), country music guitarist, record producer, and innovator.

"JOHN FERGUS RYAN ASKS POLITELY FOR A SECOND
HELPING OF BOURBON BALLS"
John Fergus Ryan (1930–2003), author of *The Redneck Bride* and two other southern novels
in the comic vein, consummate literary artist and fine conversationalist, neighbor and friend.

"DEFINITION OF TERMS"
The Stax Museum of American Soul Music, the Stax Music Academy, and The Soulsville
Charter School may be supported through the Soulsville Foundation, a 501(c)3 nonprofit.

"FORTUNE TELLER"
For Linda Raiteri, with thanks.

"ANDERSONVILLE MEMENTO"
My knowledge of the 7th Tennessee Volunteer Cavalry (USA) and their imprisonment at
Andersonville, Georgia, during the Civil War has come down to me as family lore. A more
credible source is Peggy Scott Holley's carefully researched *Hawkins' Tories: A Regimental and
Social History of the 7th Tennessee Volunteer Cavalry USA.*

CPSIA information can be obtained
at www.ICGtesting.com
Printed in the USA
LVHW032035220222
711687LV00004B/445